P9-CIS-732

MULTIPLE SCLEROSIS

WITHDRAWN

MULTIPLE SCLEROSIS

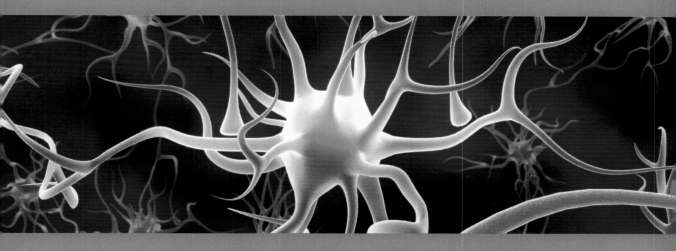

Marlene Targ Brill

Marshall Cavendish
Benchmark
New York

Special thanks to Suzi, Hillary, and Michael for sharing their stories with dignity, courage, and humor.

Marshall Cavendish Benchmark
99 White Plains Road
Tarrytown, New York 10591-9001
www.marshallcavendish.us

Text copyright © 2008 by Marshall Cavendish Corporation

All rights reserved. No part of this book may be reproduced or utilized in any form or by any means electronic or mechanical including photocopying, recording, or by any information storage and retrieval system, without permission from the copyright holders.

This book is not intended for use as a substitute for advice, consultation, or treatment by a licensed medical practitioner. The reader is advised that no action of a medical nature should be taken without consultation with a licensed medical practitioner, including action that may seem to be indicated by the contents of this work, since individual circumstances vary and medical standards, knowledge, and practices change with time. The publisher, author, and medical consultants disclaim all liability and cannot be held responsible for any problems that may arise from use of this book.

Library of Congress Cataloging-in-Publication Data

Brill, Marlene Targ.
  Multiple sclerosis / by Marlene Targ Brill.
    p. cm. -- (Health alert)
  Summary: "Discusses Multiple Sclerosis and its effects on people and society"--Provided by publisher.
  Includes bibliographical references and index.
  ISBN 978-0-7614-2699-8
  1. Multiple sclerosis--Juvenile literature. I. Title. II. Series.

  RC377.B78 2008
  616.8'34--dc22

                         2007008789

Front cover: A brain affected by Multiple Sclerosis
Title page: Nerve cells

Photo research by Candlepants Incorporated
Front cover: Mehau Kulyk / Photo Researchers
The photographs in this book are used by permission and through the courtesy of: Photo Researchers: hybrid medical animation, 3, 14; Dr. John Zajicek, 5, 17; Joubert, 13; Steve Gschmeissner, 15; CNRI, 19; Scott Camazine, 20; Cordelia Molloy, 27; Mark Thomas, 32; Living Art Enterprises, LLC, 34; James King-Holmes, 39; AJPhoto, 40, 56; Phanie, 44, 45. Corbis: Bettmann, 28; Guido Benschop/Reuters, 51; Isaac Menashe/ZUMA, 54. The Image Works: Bill Bachmann, 24; Christopher Fitzgerald, 50; Rhoda Sidney, 53. Phototake USA: BSIP, 36.
Printed in China
6 5 4 3 2 1

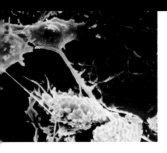

CONTENTS

1

WHAT IS IT LIKE TO HAVE MULTIPLE SCLEROSIS?

Multiple Sclerosis (MS) is an illness that strikes each person differently. Robin first noticed something wrong shortly after she turned twenty-six. In the middle of a family party, her vision became blurry. The next day, her husband drove her to an eye doctor. After an exam, the doctor confirmed that her eyesight had become worse. Eye doctors use numbers to determine how good a person's eyesight is, with 20-20 being perfect vision. Robin's eyesight had gone from a perfect 20-20 to a very cloudy 20-400. The doctor said her problem was an inflamed eye nerve that required medication and rest. After two weeks, Robin's eyesight returned to normal. She assumed the problem was an isolated, or one-time, event.

A year later, Robin experienced another unusual event. When she leaned against a cold object, she felt cold on one side of her stomach but not on the other. This time, she went to her regular doctor, who put her through several tests. The tests offered few results but pointed toward a couple of different diseases. As the doctor explained each, Robin only heard him say multiple sclerosis (MS), a disease that affects the **nervous system.** Since the nervous system includes the brain and the **spinal cord,** a collection of nerve tissue running down a person's back, Robin was scared. "As soon as you hear MS, your mind jumps to the worst cases, the ones in wheelchairs," she said.

Robin's fear of having MS came true. But her illness followed its own path and not into a wheelchair. At first, the doctor only treated her individual attacks, or flare-ups, such as the blurred vision and the numbness in her stomach. Five years passed before she experienced another attack and more numbness. After that, flare-ups came more closely together and involved other parts of her body. She felt tingling in her arms and legs and her handwriting worsened. Robin also became tired more easily. "All of sudden I couldn't walk to my daughter's school down the block," Robin said. "To the touch, my feet felt okay. But my brain wasn't sending information to my leg to move."

Robin found that one of the worst challenges with MS was being unable to predict when and where attacks would come. "Sometimes, I've had to leave work, which can be a problem,"

Robin, who is a speech teacher, recalled. "One time, I had an attack in May and went for a job interview in August. I worried that I would get a tour of the school, and I would become too tired to finish."

The doctor tried several medications to ease Robin's attacks and prevent others. Each medication triggered different side effects. "One time, the drug made me really mean. I swore at my daughter, and I never swear. My irrational behavior affected her for a while."

Robin feared for the health of her two daughters more than for her own safety. Would she pass MS onto them? Would her being sick cause them to feel bad? Could she still be the mother she wanted to be when she could not control what and when her body refused to perform?

Twice after an attack, Robin went into the hospital to receive massive doses of medication. After the second hospital stay, the doctor recommended that Robin inject herself with stronger medication every other day. This plan was challenging. In the beginning, the shots made Robin feel like she had the flu. In addition, the medication needed to be kept cold, or it would spoil. "I took a little ice pack with medication to my daughter's traveling softball games. Whenever we traveled, I rushed to find an ice bucket for the medication as soon as we arrived at a hotel. What a pain!" Robin said.

For three years, Robin or her husband injected the medication into her thigh, stomach, arms, and rear. Then she developed hard, puffy spots at the spots where the injections were. The doctor took her off that medication and Robin decided to try living without any medication. "Overall, I've been very fortunate. I haven't had a flare-up in two years. I try to be positive and not worry about the next attack."

LARRY'S STORY

Larry has not been as lucky. While his flare-ups came and went like Robin's, his **symptoms,** or signs of the illness, worsened with each attack. In between the attacks, some symptoms never left.

Larry's first flare-up occurred during army training camp when he was nineteen. While resting after stressful exercises, he realized he could not stand up again. He tried to stand up, but either his legs buckled or he became so dizzy he threw up. At first, the doctor at the army hospital thought an ear infection caused Larry's dizziness. When his ears looked clear, the doctor seemed stumped. Larry stayed in the hospital for about a month until his symptoms eased, but they could not find a reason for his problem. "I kept falling during a two-mile run," Larry said. "I had drop foot, which meant my leg dragged. Messages from my brain to my leg were blocked. I could only move part of the way, so I tripped and fell. I was bleeding by the end of the run. I finished it, got to bed, and my problem disappeared once I rested."

A year later, Larry had another attack. He became dizzy and his drop foot returned. He could not go to the bathroom when he felt the need. This time, he found a doctor who ordered the right tests. The doctor discovered that Larry had MS. Larry was shocked because he thought that most people who got MS were women older than he was.

Since he found out about MS, Larry has experienced a flare-up at least once a year. Sometimes, attacks strike three times a year. During the attacks, his vision worsens, he limps badly, and he has problems going to the bathroom. With each attack, Larry has to have a nurse come to his home to give him injections of medication. "The medication is so strong you can taste it once the needle goes into the arm. When the drug is first started, I eat peanut butter to take the terrible taste away."

Larry does not let his MS get in the way of his life. He fell in love with his nurse, married her, and together they have four children. He tries to keep a normal schedule. Larry runs his own landscaping business and he plays basketball to exercise. But his disease is worsening. His hand always feels numb and he cannot walk very well with only about 10 percent of the normal strength left in his legs. At times, severe tiredness overwhelms him. At basketball games, he cannot stand up by the end of a game. "Symptoms are worse when I get hot. Sometimes, I have to stop playing basketball. Other players give me a hard time because I play poorly, and I'm usually a pretty good player," Larry said.

Still, Larry refuses to tell anyone outside the family about his disease. He rejects the idea of a handicapped sticker for his car, so he can park closer to places. He wants to live a "normal" life. "I don't want MS to be the issue," he said. Larry fights his disease with exercise and the latest medication. Soon he will start a new type of medication, one commonly used to treat cancer. Doctors hope that it is strong enough to kill whatever attacks the nervous system and causes life-altering symptoms. But the drug is so powerful that Larry must be monitored regularly to make sure the drug never kills healthy parts of his body. Even with the dangers, Larry views this drug as hope. Larry's MS flare-ups need to become more stable and he wants his symptoms to improve. He has children to play with and basketball hoops to shoot.

2

WHAT IS MULTIPLE SCLEROSIS?

Multiple sclerosis is a mysterious disease of the nervous system. No one knows for sure what produces the attacks and flare-ups related to MS. Once flare-ups occur, symptoms of the disease may come, go, or change without warning. Symptoms can affect the same or different parts of the body each time an attack erupts. They can be as mild as numbness or as challenging as being unable to move at all.

The good news is that MS is not contagious, which means you cannot catch it like a cold or the flu. Also, most people with MS live a natural life span. Many questions remain, however, about symptoms that cannot be predicted. Scientists are still exploring causes of MS and how to cure the attacks. Fortunately, they have discovered what happens inside the body when people experience this nervous system disease.

A HEALTHY NERVOUS SYSTEM

The nervous system is made up of the brain, the spinal cord, and a network of nerves spread throughout the body. The brain houses the message center that tells the rest of the body what to do. Inside the brain are billions of nerve cells, which are tiny units of living matter that can only be seen under a microscope. Nerve cells carry messages back and forth from the brain, into the spine, and to other parts of the body. They do this through a complex network of nerve fibers. These fibers connect the brain to muscles, skin, organs, and senses throughout the body.

Different parts of the network control specific functions, such as hand movements, breathing, and seeing. For example, when you touch something hot, nerves in your

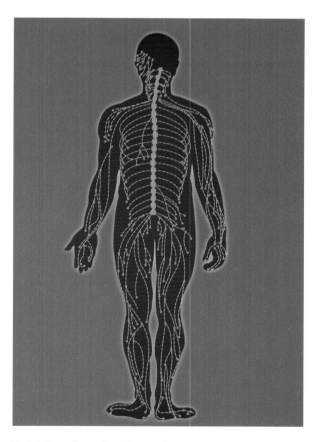

Multiple sclerosis affects the nervous system, which includes the brain, spinal cord, and nerves.

fingers send a message of pain through the nervous system. In turn, your body responds by pulling your hand away from whatever is causing the painful sensations. By sending messages to and from the brain and spinal cord, nerves help us perform a range of behaviors, so we can move, talk, think, and sense our environment.

In healthy people, messages shoot up and back along the nervous system at lightning speeds. Scientists estimate that the messages move at about 225 miles per hour. Usually, we never

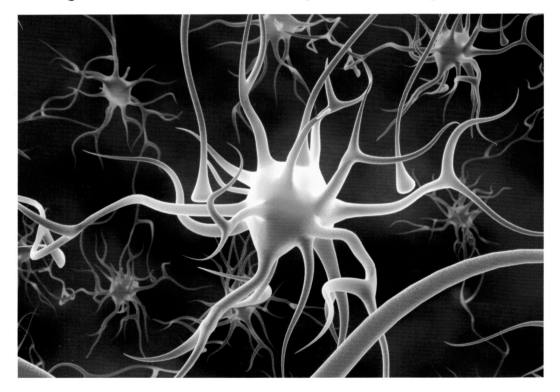

A healthy network of nerves is able to send and receive messages throughout the body.

notice how our nervous system works. To us, it just works automatically, much like flipping a switch just turns on a light.

To help nerves perform their job, they are encased in a fatty material called **myelin.** The myelin sheath, or cover, protects nerves as they relay messages. This is similar to rubber casing around electrical wires. This covering insures that high-speed messages travel directly to where they should go. That way, a healthy person can perform a variety of daily activities as needed.

A NERVOUS SYSTEM WITH MS

Nerves of people with MS do not function properly. Damage to the myelin sheath—such as fraying or blockage—interferes with smooth trans-mission of messages to and from the brain and spinal cord. This damage is called **demyelination** and blocks signals to or from a certain part of the body. Sometimes signals become distorted, causing events such as blurred vision or unsteady walking. Other times signals

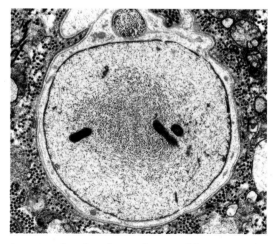

A nerve that has been damaged by MS, such as this one, lacks the thick protective coating that keeps it healthy.

are totally interrupted, as with blindness or the inability to move the legs at all. That is why one person with MS may lose eyesight, while another feels weak or numb in the hands or feet. If the damage is great, complete nerve loss may develop.

As MS progresses, hard patches of tissue grow over the damaged areas. These patches create visible scars on the brain and spine. The name multiple sclerosis comes from this scarring. *Sclerosis* is the Greek term for "scarring," and "multiple" refers to the many scars that can occur throughout the nervous system.

What Causes Demyelination?

Scientists believe damage to the myelin results from a mistake in the **immune system.** The immune system is the human body's way of protecting itself against disease. When a foreign substance enters the body, the immune system sends out an army of cells to destroy the invader. For example, when flu germs threaten health, special cells identify the flu viruses and destroy them or make them harmless.

Sometimes, the immune system army makes a mistake. Healthy cells or necessary parts of the body are wrongly identified as intruders. The immune system attacks these intruders,

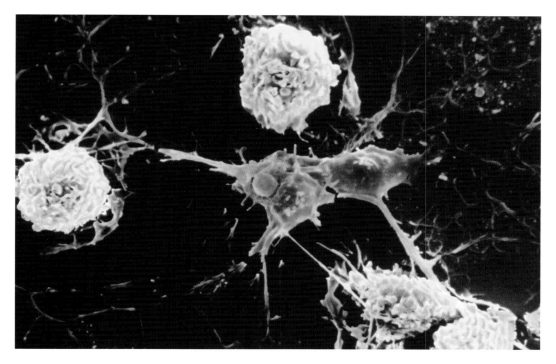

Nerves deteriorate because cells in the body attack them. This magnified image shows immune cells (yellow) destroying healthy cells (pink) that form a nerve's myelin sheath.

even though they are not causing problems. A disease that causes the immune system to attack healthy parts of the body is called an **autoimmune disease.** With MS, the immune system attacks the body's own myelin. Wherever the attack takes place, myelin gets destroyed. Breaks in nerve communication follow, and signs of MS result. More signs of MS develop as more areas are attacked. Once a mistake—such as identifying myelin as an intruder—happens, the attacks seem to continue. Most often, they persist for the rest of a person's life.

Why does the body attack itself? No one knows for sure. Perhaps the immune system thinks myelin cells resemble other, more dangerous cells. Or something in the environment, such as a virus, sparks the error. This is one of many pieces in the MS puzzle yet to be solved.

TYPES OF MS

MS progresses differently for each person with the disease. Symptoms can be mild, moderate, or severe. They may come and go without a pattern or slowly worsen after the first flare-up. According to the National Multiple Sclerosis Society, doctors usually define MS by one of these four main paths of the disease.

Relapsing-Remitting

The most common form of MS involves **relapses,** or occasional flare-ups, and remitting, which refers to periods without symptoms. About 85 percent of people with MS experience bouts of one or more signs followed by a period of complete or near-complete recovery, which is called remission. Each flare-up causes swelling around the place where myelin is destroyed. This swelling is similar to what we experience after cutting our skin. Only with MS, swelling blocks messages sent through the nerves, which triggers symptoms.

Once swelling eases, nerves conduct messages again, which relieves the symptoms.

The cycle of relapses and remitting continues until nerves become so damaged they cannot work properly. Relapses usually occur every few years or a couple of times a year. After a

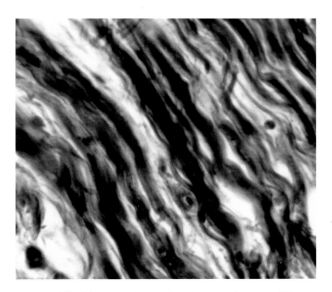

A magnified image shows the damaged nerve fibers (black) that are affected by MS. The white spaces are areas where the myelin has been destroyed.

while, however, nerve damage may progress to the point that symptoms appear more often with fewer, if any, disease-free periods. Then MS follows a more severe path of disease.

Secondary-Progressive

About one in every two people who have relapsing-remitting MS develops the secondary-progressive form of the disease. With secondary-progressive MS, symptoms worsen either with or without returning periods of recovery. Once MS has progressed to this stage, symptoms during recovery periods never truly go away. They usually worsen with time.

Primary-Progressive

One in ten people who have MS find their illness slowly worsens after the first attack. Every person may experience a different rate of progression or advancement of the disease, and symptoms may level off for awhile. But people with primary-progressive MS never undergo periods of remission that give them a break without symptoms.

Progressive-Relapsing

This rare form of MS progresses steadily from the first

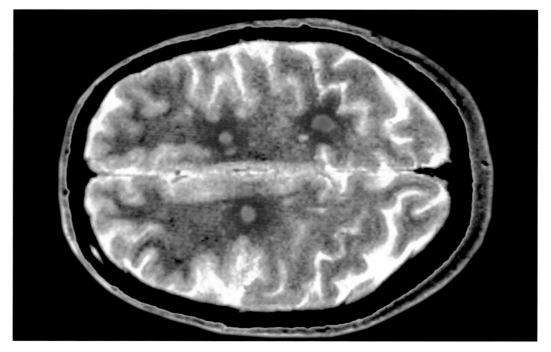

MS can eventually spread to the brain, where it damages brain tissue. This scan shows brain damage (pink spots) in the brain of a person with MS.

flare-ups and erupts into unexpected attacks. The attacks may or may not worsen the disease. But between the attacks, MS continues to advance. The speed of advancing depends upon the individual.

Between 10 and 20 percent of people with MS find that their illness disappears completely after the first attack. Either the disease never progresses, or damage to the nervous system appears in places that do not interfere with functioning. In rare cases, however, once MS strikes, it progresses quickly. Within a short time, the sufferer becomes disabled in areas touched by the disease.

MS TRIGGERS

Doctors try to pinpoint what affects the course of the illness. Infections, such as flu, colds, and other severe illnesses, raise the risk of relapse. So does physical and emotional stress. People with MS can play sports, but doctors caution against activities that cause extreme fatigue, such as running in races. Heat worsens symptoms for 60 percent of people with MS. The heat can come from outside the body or inside from exercising. In these situations, symptoms usually disappear once the body cools.

Another factor for women with MS involves having a baby. Studies show that MS symptoms may become more stable or improve while a woman is pregnant. But attacks occur for 20 to 40 percent of the women within three months after delivering the baby. Having a baby does not seem to affect the course of the disease overall.

WHO GETS MS?

Reports estimate that more than 400,000 people in the United States have MS. Doctors report about two hundred new cases every week. Many more remain undiscovered partly because of the difficulty in identifying a disease that comes, goes, and changes with time. There is also a lack of tests that pinpoint origins of symptoms.

Most people notice the first signs of MS between ages twenty and forty. For unknown reasons, gender and environment play a role in who gets MS. Women experience MS at more than twice the rate of men, particularly at younger ages. As adults age, however, this imbalance in the number of new cases levels off.

New cases of MS are five times more likely to occur in colder regions than in hot. Multiple sclerosis rates are higher in the northern United States, Canada, and Europe than in places with year-round tropical climates. Studies show that people who move from tropical regions to cold climates before the age of fifteen increase their risk of developing MS. Teens who move from tropical to cold after the age of fifteen do not increase their chances, and instead maintain the same level of risk as other people in their homeland.

These findings suggest that environment plays a role in developing MS. But researchers still scratch their heads about exactly what in the environment leads to MS. Is it temperature, less sunshine, rainfall, or altitude? Or do people in these regions eat different foods or mingle with others in large cities where more germs lurk? The MS puzzle continues.

Another risk factor for MS is ethnic background. Asians, Inuits, and Africans rarely have MS. But white people from northern Europe and their children make up most of the cases of the disease. Slightly higher numbers of cases run in families. Children of parents who have MS face fifteen to twenty times the risk of getting the disease as the general population. Although total numbers of MS cases are small, MS is the most common disease of the nervous system.

CHILDREN WITH MS

At one time, doctors believed MS only struck adults. Now they know this is not true. About 10,000 of the 400,000 patients

Like adults, children with MS can show a variety of symptoms. Though MS has caused this child to use a wheelchair, he is still able to attend public school with other students his age.

with MS in the United States are children. Many believe the numbers are actually higher because signs of MS may go unrecognized in children. Once studies claimed that cases of MS appeared between ages ten and seventeen. Now doctors find that children as young as four can show MS signs. Even worse, doctors see the number of new MS cases in children rising.

SYMPTOMS

People with MS can display a range of symptoms. Some signs appear obvious to someone else, such as trouble walking or talking. Other symptoms, such as tingling and memory loss, are invisible to others. Not everyone with MS experiences all of these problems. Each case is individual. Here are some of the most common signs of MS reported by the National Multiple Sclerosis Society:

- Tingling
- Dizziness
- Weakness
- Tiredness
- Numbness
- Pain
- Loss of balance
- Cramps or tense muscles
- Inability to move arms or legs

- Blurred or jumpy vision
- Problems going to the bathroom
- Changes in emotional behavior
- Changes in memory, thinking, and attention
- Difficulty making decisions
- Headaches
- Problems speaking or swallowing

3

THE HISTORY OF MULTIPLE SCLEROSIS

Cases of multiple sclerosis probably go back to the beginning of time. But people long ago left few writings about illness. If they did, they never connected the varied symptoms of MS to one disease. Centuries went by before the field of medicine as we know it today emerged. During that time, individuals who were ill relied on a mixture of home remedies, witchcraft, and superstition for their health care.

FIRST REPORTS OF MS

The earliest written record of MS came from accounts beginning in 1395. Count Jan Van Bieren of Holland wrote about a Dutch woman named Lidwina of Scheidam who suffered from unexplained illness. Van Bieren described the fifteen-year-old's terrible face pain. He told how she developed leg weakness that caused her to fall while ice skating, which was

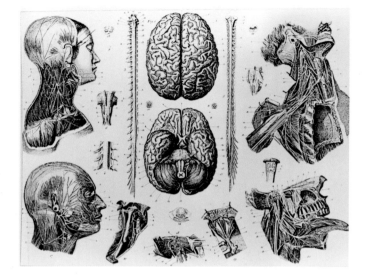

Until they learned more about the nervous system and how it worked, scientists could not explain certain behaviors that we now know are associated with MS. These medical illustration of the different parts of the nervous system were drawn in the 1850s.

a sport that she loved. As Lidwina grew older, Van Bieren documented her frequent inability to walk, feel her legs, and see out of one eye. The Count marveled, however, at how Lidwina always helped others despite her suffering. After she died in 1433 at age fifty-three, monks submitted her name for sainthood. She became the Saint of Ice Skaters.

Four centuries later, while inspecting dead bodies, doctors noticed unusual changes in the brain and spinal cord. A few questioned whether small brown and white patches along the nervous system related to unexplained symptoms in their patients. But they never connected the patches with a specific disease.

In 1868, Jean-Martin Charcot, a noted professor at the University of Paris, linked changes in the brain with signs of

MS. Between 1862 and 1870, he examined thousands of patients at a Paris institution for people who were poor, old, or sick. His reports confirmed that signs of MS came from changes in the nervous system he noticed after his patients died. He wrote about *la sclerose en plaques,* or "scarring in patches" that alters the way the nervous system functions.

Charcot's discoveries eventually led to a better understanding of the disease.

ODD THEORIES

Charcot tried several treatments to ease the course of MS in his patients. He injected them with gold and silver. He shocked them with electricity or gave them poison to stimulate the nervous system.

Other doctors tried their own treatments. None knew for sure what caused the symptoms, so they experimented. One doctor believed MS resulted from the body's inability to sweat properly.

He gave his patients medication to generate fevers that made them sweat a lot. Those who believed MS came from too much exercise recommended bed rest and herbs. Doctors who thought MS resulted from unknown poison in the blood gave their patients medications to make them vomit or have bowel movements that removed the poison from the body. None of these treatments cured MS.

NEW DISCOVERIES

French doctor Louis Ranvier identified the body's myelin in 1878. His description of nervous system features led other scientists to look more closely at how the nervous system worked. In 1925, British scientist Lord Edgar Adrian began a series of experiments that recorded the first electrical activity in nerves. His studies established how nerves conducted messages to and from the brain. Adrian confirmed the role of myelin in these transmissions and what happens when points along a nerve swell and block pathways.

By the 1920s, doctors knew that MS was present in abnormal fluid from the spine. But they had no clue what that meant in terms of the cause or cure. At that time, the commonly held opinion was that men suffered more from MS than women. Doctors thought that MS symptoms in women were from hysteria, or extreme nervousness or madness. This thinking has since been reversed.

In 1935, Dr. Thomas Rivers reproduced a form of MS in lab animals. Rivers's experiment found that nerve problems, rather than an outside agent such as a virus, produced signs of MS. These findings led to current thinking about MS as an autoimmune disease.

For the next two decades, doctors focused on allergies as the reason MS occurred. They treated patients with allergy-curbing drugs and vitamins. But patients continued to experience the same symptoms and varied progression of the disease. Fortunately, some things improved, such as better hospital care and infection control. As a result, all people lived longer life spans, including patients with MS.

More recently, doctors confirmed the belief that in MS, the body's immune system goes haywire and attacks its own myelin. Researchers continue to investigate why. Several studies target family history. According to the National Multiple Sclerosis Society, the average person in the United States has a 1 in 750 risk of developing the disease. Having a brother, sister, or parent with MS raises chances to between 1 in 100 and 1 in 40. Being an identical twin who shares the same makeup as someone with MS boosts risk to 1 in 4. Studies show that identical twins reared in different families miles apart face this same risk, proving that there is a link between family and MS. Though the risk increases with twins, one twin having MS does not mean that the other will definitely get it.

Since identical twins are not equally at risk, scientists believe other factors besides family medical history contribute to MS. Researchers continue to study families with more than one case of MS, including their environments and their ethnic background. Other studies focus on customs and habits, such as smoking or job environments.

Researchers are beginning to look at MS in children. The first report of a child with MS appeared in 1980. Since then, the number of cases has risen steadily, creating a need for research into how MS effects children. Investigators hope that studies of children can pinpoint disease triggers.

Younger patients have been exposed to fewer factors, such as viruses, than older patients, which helps with research. Studies indicate that 53 percent of children with MS are African American or Hispanic. This tells researchers to focus on specific environments and backgrounds as possible triggers. Still, many unknowns remain. Besides learning what causes immune system mistakes, scientists struggle with how to identify MS earlier and how to eliminate the disease.

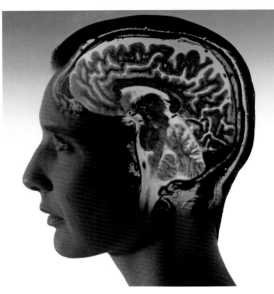

Better understanding of the brain and spinal cord has led to easier diagnosis and improved treatments.

IDENTIFYING MS TODAY

No single test detects MS. Instead, doctors use a series of steps to rule out other disorders. They look for outward signs of the disease in parts of the nervous system. They have the patient record at least two separate flare-ups.

Even with these guidelines, identifying MS can be difficult. Damage to the nervous system is largely invisible. So doctors rely on a combination of personal accounts, lab tests, and new technology to confirm disease. The process can go smoothly, with MS discovered easily. Or detecting MS can take months or years. During a long, drawn-out process, worried patients and their families often become discouraged.

Medical History

One tool doctors use to verify MS involves acquiring a complete health picture of the patient. Doctors want to know about someone's symptoms. They also need information about previous illnesses, medications, and family history of nervous system diseases. Doctors who suspect but cannot confirm MS may ask the patient to keep a diary. Diaries help doctors pinpoint the disease and highlight specific symptoms to reduce.

Examination

Doctors perform a general physical exam to check for other illnesses and signs of MS. They check the heart, chest, and muscles and skin. If findings point to a problem with the nervous system, family doctors usually refer patients to a **neurologist,** a doctor who specializes in problems of the nervous system. Neurologists test for coordination, sensations, and strength. They evaluate face and eye movements. Results of these activities determine whether the neurologist orders further nerve tests.

Magnetic Resonance Imaging (MRI)

An important tool in detecting MS is magnetic resonance imaging (MRI). This photographic scanner takes pictures of different inside parts of the body. Undergoing an MRI is painless, but the patient must lie very still inside a tube-like scanner. A magnet in the machine scans the body and sends information to a computer. The computer translates the magnetic information into pictures that display portions of the brain, spinal cord, or other parts of the body.

Doctors began using MRI scans for MS in 1984. Scientists noticed that these photographed slices of the brain revealed MS attacks. By 1988, series of MRI scans showed how the disease progressed. An MRI series also confirmed that MS progresses even without symptoms. Today, doctors use MRI scans to locate patches in the nervous system that result from myelin loss.

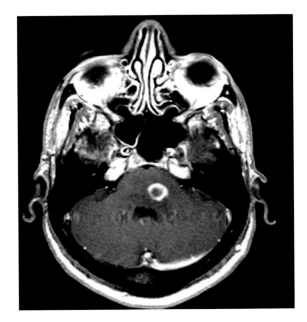

Magnetic resonance imaging technology has helped in identifying MS. But this form of imaging is not perfect. In 25 percent of MS cases, the disease is not visible through MRI scans. Also, the pattern of what the scans show may be the same as patterns in other diseases unrelated to MS. To confirm results, doctors often order other tests.

Evoked Potential Test

This test measures how quickly and correctly the nervous

system responds. Wires are placed on the patient's head, neck, and limbs. These wires are connected to a computer that will record the results. The patient's hearing, feeling, and seeing nerve pathways are then stimulated. For example, to test eye nerves the patient may be asked to watch a pattern on a television monitor. As the patient responds to these stimuli, the computer records the responses. The doctors then look at the results to see how quickly the patient responded to different stimuli.

If MS is involved, demyelination causes nerve signals to slow, and the results of the test will reflect this. Doctors recommend these tests when the MRI fails to confirm MS or results of other tests are borderline, which means there is no definite answer.

Evoked potential tests are less expensive than MRI scans, and they detect early MS in 65 percent of the cases. Additionally, the evoked potential tests are not very painful. During these tests, the patient may feel tingling in the arms or legs when the parts are excited.

Spinal Tap

Fluid that surrounds the brain and spinal cord—called cerebrospinal fluid or CSF—yields information about several health conditions, including MS. If doctors suspect MS and still cannot confirm the illness, they may order a spinal tap. This test involves testing a sample of CSF. The fluid sample is sent to a lab to be studied for signs of MS.

This test is more invasive than MRIs or evoked potential tests. To remove the fluid, a doctor inserts a long needle into the patient's back. Patients must stay very still for this test. Sometimes they complain of discomfort during the test. Afterward, they must lie flat on their stomachs so that the needle site will close and CSF fluids in the spine can even out. Those who sit up too quickly may get a headache.

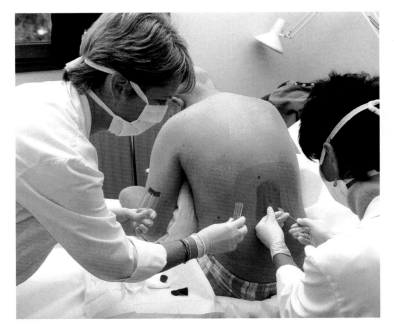

A doctor and nurse take a sample of CSF from this patient's spine. The fluid will be tested for disease like MS.

MYTHS AND FACTS

MYTH: Many people who have MS look healthy, so they must be using their disease as an excuse to get out of work.

FACT: Just because someone looks healthy does not mean that they are not experiencing traces of MS. Some people with MS suffer unseen signs, such as extreme tiredness, numbness, blurred vision, and nerve pain.

MYTH: You can catch MS from someone else.

FACT: Multiple sclerosis is not contagious. You cannot get MS by kissing, touching, or being near someone who has the disease.

MYTH: People with MS die within a short time.

FACT: People with MS rarely die from the disease. Most live as long as people without the disease.

MYTH: All people with MS need wheelchairs to move around.

FACT: MS affects each person differently. Some people with MS become so severely disabled that they require a wheelchair, but not everyone is like this. At times, flare-ups cause weakness or poor coordination. A wheelchair insures they can move about safely until the attack ends. For individuals with advanced MS, a wheelchair provides transportation.

4

LIVING WITH MULTIPLE SCLEROSIS

For now, no cure exists for MS. Treatment centers on discovering, or diagnosing, the illness early and relieving or preventing harmful autoimmune responses. But other areas of life may change when MS strikes. Therefore, good treatment considers a person's mental as well as physical health.

TREATMENT OF PHYSICAL SYMPTOMS

Improved methods to identify MS and target medication give people with this disease tools to combat their symptoms. This was not always true. Until the 1990s, lasting medical treatments for MS were only dreams. In 1993, scientists created the first drug that altered the course of MS. Since then, new drugs have been developed to reduced the size of demyelinated patches and prevent new tears and growths in myelin covering.

Treatment varies based upon the kind of MS someone has. Doctors treat periodic relapses differently from disease that continues to worsen over time. People who have sudden, serious attacks may go into the hospital for high doses of **corticosteroids.** Nurses inject this medication directly into the vein. The drug acts quickly to reduce swelling and immune system responses. Corticosteroids work well for the short term. But they have little impact on preventing other attacks or long-term recovery. Corticosteroids can also cause serious side effects, so doctors monitor their use carefully.

Several newer medications target symptoms that come and go. The most popular types are **interferon beta** and **glatiramer acetate.** Patients usually inject the drugs themselves daily, every other day, or weekly. These medications were the first to help adjust the immune system and delay advancing disease. They are not a cure, however.

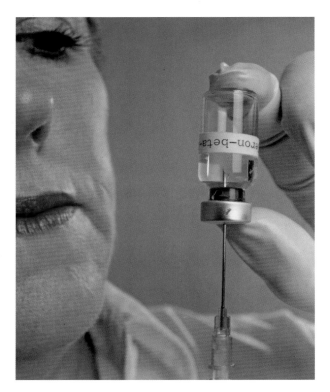

Injectable drugs have had an enormous effect on treating people with MS.

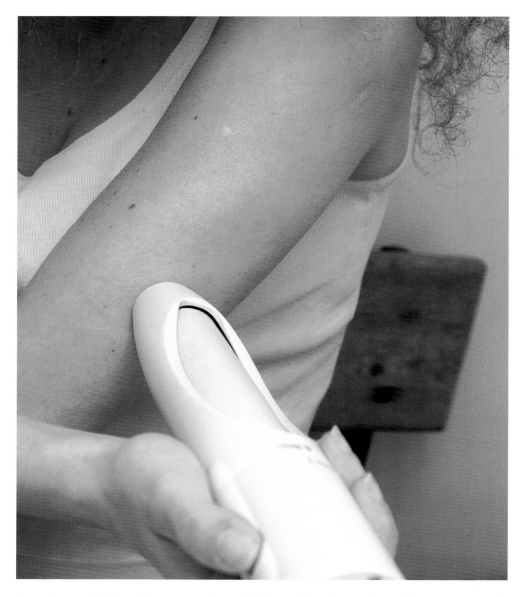

Many forms of MS medication can be administered by the patient. This makes it easier, since he or she would not need to go to a doctor's office to receive treatments.

And people who take them may experience side effects. The most common side effects include chills, fever, muscle aches, and tiredness. To prevent more serious problems, patients who use these drugs must have their blood tested regularly.

Some symptoms refuse to respond to any drugs. Researchers are studying a range of new treatments for severe MS. A few drugs used to treat cancer are being tested in some types of MS. These drugs attack diseased cells, but they also attack surrounding healthy cells. Attacks on healthy cells produce terrible side effects, including cancer. So use of these drugs has to be carefully monitored.

Other treatment options besides medications are being studied. One study involves injecting MS patients with cell-building substances found in bones of a healthy donor. Another study investigates drawing blood from the patient, cleaning the blood, and putting it back into the bloodstream. The hope is that the healthy blood will overcome whatever triggers an autoimmune response.

For many people with MS, medication is their lifeline. Others find they function well without the drugs. Their symptoms are mild, and they rarely interrupt daily living. These people believe that the serious side effects from medication are worse than MS symptoms. So they choose to take their chances and not take any drugs.

Medication for Children

Many children and their parents go to doctors who believe only adults get MS. As a result, children with symptoms may go untreated for years. Even when doctors know how to recognize MS in children, no guidelines exist for how to help their young patients. Drug testing usually focuses on adults. Study results provide no proof that these drugs work or are safe for children. Questions arise about whether MS drugs stunt a child's growth, which is something that does not affect adults.

Doctors prescribe the same medications for children anyway. They believe that it would be worse to do nothing and let repeated attacks damage the brain and advance the disease. So far, adult medications for MS have shown few added side effects for children. But giving these drugs to children is considered too new to say they are definitely safe.

MANAGING SPECIFIC SYMPTOMS

Over the years, patients and their doctors have tried various treatments to ease symptoms of MS. Some treatments, such as injecting snake poison, proved dangerous. Other questionable treatments have included applying electric current to the spinal cord, removing silver or mercury tooth fillings, or implanting a pig brain into the patient's belly through surgery. None of these treatments worked. There are, however, some other ways that patients can try to treat their symptoms.

Controlling Diet

Every few years, a researcher links MS to diet. Some doctors tell their patients to eat a low-fat diet, while others promote eating fats found in safflower, primrose, and sunflower seed oil. Patients have been told to swallow large doses of vitamins, particularly B12 or C. They have also been encouraged to follow diets without sugar and **gluten,** an elastic substance found in grains such as wheat, rye, and barley.

As of today, studies have never confirmed that any of these diets help lessen symptoms of MS. Usually, doctors tell patients with MS what they tell anyone: Control body weight to reduce strain on weak limbs. Eat a balanced diet that includes large amounts of fruit, vegetables, and grains. Stay away from alcohol and cigarettes.

Improving Balance and Coordination

Sometimes, MS causes muscles to contract or stiffen. In these cases, doctors recommend specific medications to relax muscles. In addition to medication, doctors may refer patients to a **physical therapist.** Trained physical therapists put patients through a series of movements and exercises that improve use of bones, muscles, and joints.

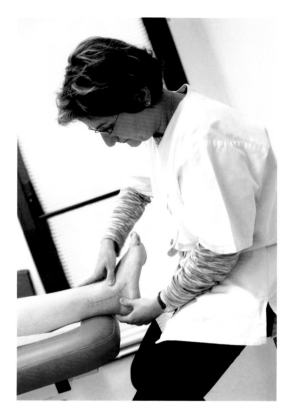

Patients learn to perform some exercises on their own. Stretching reduces muscle stiffness. Lifting weights strengthens muscles. Conditioning exercise, such as walking, boosts general fitness by increasing heart

Physical therapy is also used for people who have had certain injuries or are recovering from surgeries.

and breathing rates. People with MS who exercise at home must guard against getting overheated, which may trigger attacks. Periods of rest, cool drinks, ice packs, and air conditioning can prevent overheating. Swimming is particularly good conditioning exercise for people with MS. Water supports weak muscles and cools a heat-sensitive body.

Several devices offer people with MS ways to move about when walking becomes too difficult. Walkers and canes help steady balance and moving. Wheelchairs and electric scooters provide transportation for people whose legs refuse to work correctly.

Some people cannot accept wheelchairs and scooters. They either deny that they are sick enough, or they find them a sign of weakness or giving into their

Most people with serious forms of MS use wheelchairs. Some wheelchairs have special remote-control devices to move them forward.

disease. But such forms of transportation can actually free a person to handle more daily activities independently.

Handling Tiredness

Extreme tiredness is the most common complaint with MS.

People with the illness tire easily during activity. They may regain their energy or suddenly feel totally drained and unable to function for days or weeks. Making sure someone does not become too tired involves planning ahead. Activities that are strenuous and heat-producing require planned rest periods before symptoms arise. Planning includes using aids to replace weak limbs and following tips that reduce physical stress. Many patients benefit from arranging their day so the most tiring activities occur during peak energy hours, such as shortly after waking. They avoid heating pads, hot tubs, and hot lights. They find relief in making a list that orders the most important tasks and doing those first. Tasks lower on the list are left for a time when energy improves.

Reducing Pain

Almost half of all people with MS experience some form of pain besides the discomforts that accompany normal aging. MS pains can be sharp jabs to the face, shooting limb pains, aching muscles, or burning and tingling. Besides medication, aches and pains can be reduced by physical **therapy,** stretching exercises, and relaxation techniques such as deep breathing and refocusing thoughts onto something pleasant. Massage, cold packs, and over-the-counter painkillers such as aspirin help some people, though others disagree.

Stabbing face pain and headaches can be helped by targeted medicines that calm nerves that cause the discomfort. When drugs do not work, having a professional insert a fine needle into part of the face and one of the nerves usually stops the pain. In rare cases, surgery is required to cut nerves to the painful area. This option is a last resort, since surgery can result in numbing muscles in the face.

EMOTIONAL HEALTH

People who hear they have MS often struggle with a range of feelings. They may be overwhelmed by the thought of having a lifelong disease. They may fear unexpected attacks and how they will handle them. They may wonder how far their MS will progress, and if it will leave them dependent upon others for daily activities. Many people also worry about the effect their illness will have on family members. Money concerns can trigger a different set of worries. Long-term disease costs money for drugs, therapy, caregivers, and doctors. Talking about these feelings and seeking answers to questions helps.

Handling Emotions

Learning to live with MS involves understanding the disease and where to find help. Knowledge is power. People with MS handle their disease better when they know what to expect. They can take an active role in finding treatment and aids that work best for them. Information is available through the National Multiple Sclerosis Society, Multiple Sclerosis Foundation, and other groups that assist families facing nerve and autoimmune diseases. By understanding MS and the latest research, patients gain confidence that they can do something about their condition. Taking control helps strengthen self-esteem and can reduce depression.

Many people with MS find that talking about their emotions helps. Regular family meetings allow everyone to express feelings about a member who has MS. The person with MS can explain feelings and symptoms, so others know what is happening to their loved one. Children find their chance to share hidden fears, such as causing or catching their parent's MS. Kids may feel guilty about being angry at a parent who seems so unavailable or relies on them for extra chores. They may want to help but not know how. Talking together allows family members to plan ahead. They can talk about how to handle uncomfortable and embarrassing situations, such as attacks in public or in front of a child's friends. Family meetings offer an opportunity for individuals to decide together how best to share chores, help the person with MS, and find ways to have fun together as a family.

Almost all people with MS experience anxiety or depression at some time. When sadness becomes overwhelming, talking to a professional helps. Some patients benefit from joining groups with others who have MS or other long-term diseases. Others choose to stay away from groups with other MS sufferers because they do not want to see people who are in worse shape than they are. They want to focus on staying healthy. Family members may find groups for caretakers equally helpful. Local MS organizations may arrange groups for children who either have MS or have parents that do. If talking does not help, however, medication for depression may be an option.

Relieving Stress

Having an uncontrollable, long-term disease can be stressful and depressing. Both reactions contribute to flare-ups. Different techniques work to relieve stress and depression in individuals with MS. The easiest method to relax involves slow, deep rhythmic breathing. Relaxing is often a matter of mind over body. Clearing the head to focus on breathing reduces worry, which leads to relaxed muscles and a sense of well-being.

Besides deep breathing, music refocuses the mind and encourages relaxing. For people who have trouble remaining still long enough to relax, music gives them purpose.

Many people with MS do not let their disease affect activities that they like to do. Staying active and having fun can also help reduce stress and depression related to MS.

Peaceful sounds, such as ocean waves or harp music, lower muscle tension and slow blood flow and breathing.

Meditation is another way to relax. Those who meditate focus on a single word or object as a means of reaching a relaxed state. As the mind drifts, its becomes free of distracting thoughts. For many, meditation calms the body and mind, which reduces stress and relaxes muscles. Visualization is a relaxing technique similar to meditation. With visualization, the individual creates a mental picture of health, rather than focusing on a single word or object. Imagining the body in a healthy state reinforces the message that the body is strong and can heal itself. This image changes how the person perceives MS, which can have an impact on how the immune system responds to disease. Books and workshops help individuals learn how to visualize healthy pictures.

Another way some people with MS control pain and stress is by smoking or eating products made with the **cannabis** plant, which is also known as marijuana. For people with MS, cannabis can bring pain relief. It can help with tingling sensations, urgent

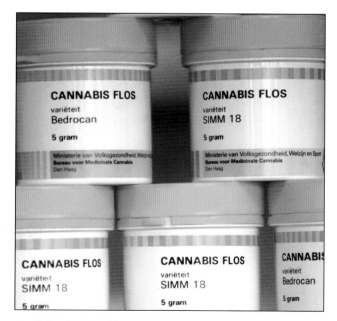

Medicinal cannabis can help ease the painful symptoms of diseases like MS.

bladder, shaky legs, and depression. That means patients need fewer medications, which saves them money. It also protects them from some of the medications' side effects. The problem is that the plant is illegal in most states. It is illegal because people who are not ill abuse marijuana as a drug. The federal government outlaws growing, selling, and ingesting marijuana no matter how much it helps with a range of diseases. However, eleven states have legalized eating or inhaling cannabis for people who have a doctor's recommendation. Efforts are under way to make marijuana legal for medical use in all states.

Working Around Thinking Problems

One in two people with MS experience problems with their ability to think, reason, and remember. About 5 to 10 percent of these people find their problems severe enough to interfere with how they function. Those with mild memory problems keep a notebook or computer-like instrument nearby to record information they do not want to forget. Writing down activities helps them organize and plan better. When MS makes performing everyday activities dangerous or impossible, the sick person may need a caretaker at home or outside the home.

This student with MS uses a special computer to help her with her schoolwork.

UNDERSTANDING DIFFERENCES IN CHILDREN

Children with MS have different concerns. Unexpected flare-ups can interfere with sports and learning in school. Most of those with MS exhibit only mild signs of the disease, but some find attacks hit five or more times a year. These result in lost school days. Going to school brings other

FAMOUS PEOPLE WITH MS

In the past, many people tried to hide their MS. Today, those with various symptoms talk about their disease. Many television shows and movies highlight people who have MS. The successes and openness of these shows and the following people give others with MS hope that they can achieve and find happiness despite illness.

Joan Sweeney, children's book author

Richard Pryor, comic and actor

Clay Walker, country music singer

Stephanie Stephans, golfer

Joan Didion, writer and director

Montel Williams, talk show host

Celebrities like Montel Williams help to bring attention to diseases like MS.

challenges. Vision that fades in and out interferes with reading. Shaky hands make writing and drawing difficult. Even the mildest symptoms can affect concentration and memory.

Parents struggle with watching their child suffer and not being able to fix the problem. But there are ways to make their child's life easier. Tutors can help students with MS keep up with their studies. Home schooling may allow for learning on the student's energy schedule without the stress of busy school hallways and classrooms. Computers that respond to voice commands can help with writing and staying in touch with friends, and magnifying devices can accommodate for poor vision.

Students may benefit from talking with other kids who have MS. Local groups can be located through MS organizations, hospitals, and other social service agencies. Most of all, parents need to keep lines of communication open with their children. This way everyone can feel comfortable talking about feelings and symptoms.

THE FUTURE

Scientists are just beginning to put pieces of the MS puzzle together. But they have a long way to go to find better ways

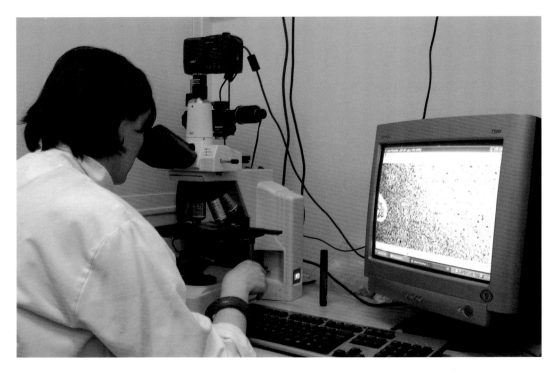

Scientists continue to develop new drugs and methods of treatment for MS.

to diagnose and treat MS. In the meantime, people with MS, like Robin, offer some suggestions about dealing with MS, "Just be positive and not worry about the next attack. Eat right and exercise. Deal with what's happening at the time. When you have moments free from MS, enjoy them and take advantage."

Her daughter, Hillary, agrees. She says of her mother, "She's really positive and helps other people deal with MS positively. She . . . practices what she preaches."

GLOSSARY

autoimmune disease—A disease that causes the immune system to attack healthy parts of the body.

cannabis—A type of plant, also called marijuana, that can be smoked or eaten to reduce certain signs of MS, but is currently illegal in most states.

corticosteroid—A type of drug that can be used to quickly reduce swelling in MS.

demyelination—Damage to the myelin that covers nerves.

glatiramer acetate—A type of drug that reduces how often MS flare-ups appear.

gluten—An elastic substance found in grains such as wheat, rye, and barley.

immune system—A network of organs, vessels, cells, and other body parts that protect the body from disease.

interferon beta—A type of drug that decreases the number of MS flare-ups.

myelin—The protective covering of nerve threads in the nervous system.

nervous system—The brain, spine, and network of nerves that transmit messages to and from the brain to different parts of the body so someone can move, think, and sense the world.

neurologist—A type of doctor who specializes in problems of the nervous system.

physical therapist—A trained professional who helps bodies move better through exercises that improve use of bones, muscles, and joints.

Primary-Progressive MS—The kind of MS in which the disease progresses after the first attack without symptom-free periods.

Progressive-Relapsing MS—A rare form of MS that progresses steadily from the first flare-up and erupts into unexpected attacks.

relapse—A period during which something—such as symptoms of a disease—reappears.

Relapse-Remitting MS—he most common type of MS, in which symptoms reappear (relapse) and go (remit).

Secondary-Progressive MS—The form of MS in which periodic symptoms become constant and more challenging.

spinal cord—Nerve tissue that runs down a person's back. The spinal cord and fluid surrounding it is protected by a column of bones known as the spine.

symptoms—Signs that indicate the presence of disease or illness.

therapy—Treatment for a problem.

FIND OUT MORE

Organizations

National Multiple Sclerosis Society
733 Third Avenue, 3rd Floor
New York, New York 10017-3288
800-344-4867 (FIGHTMS)
http://www.nationalmssociety.org

National Pediatric MS Center at Stony Brook University Hospital
Department of Neurology, HSC-T12-020
Stony Brook University
Stony Brook, New York 17794-8121
631-444-7802
http://www.pediatricmscenter.org

Multiple Sclerosis Foundation
6350 North Andrews Avenue
Ft. Lauderdale, Florida 33309-2130
888-225-6495
http://www.msfocus.org

Books

Goldstein, Margaret. *Everything You Need to Know about Multiple Sclerosis.* New York: Rosen Publishing Group, 2001.

Burnfield, Alexander. *Multiple Sclerosis.* Chicago: Heinemann Library, 2004.

Davis, Amelia. *My Story: A Photographic Essay on Life with Multiple Sclerosis.* New York: Demos Medical Publishing, 2004.

Web Sites

American Autoimmune Related Diseases Association
http://www.aarda.org

**Let's Talk MS -- for Kids
(Multiple Sclerosis Society of Canada)**
http://www.msforkids.com/index.asp

Multiple Sclerosis Association of America
http://www.msaa.com

**Multiple Sclerosis: Hope through Research
(National Institute of Neurological Disorders)**
http://www.ninds.nih.gov/disorders/multiple_sclerosis

Neuroscience for Kids -- Multiple Sclerosis
http://faculty.washington.edu/chudler/ms.html

ABOUT THE AUTHOR

With more than 65 books, Marlene Targ Brill writes about many topics from history to biographies to tooth fairies and world peace. Some favorite topics involve ways to help people become healthier. Marlene loved studying health when she was in school. She came from a family of pharmacists, who prepared and sold medicine to make people feel better. At one time, she wanted to be a nurse. Instead, she taught children who had special needs. Now she writes about special needs and other health topics for children and adults. She lives and works in a home near Chicago that she shares with her husband, Richard, her favorite reviewer.

INDEX

Page numbers for illustrations are in **boldface**

3 1901 04564 3196